Healthy Alternatives to Sweets & Snacks

Mason Crest
450 Parkway Drive, Suite D
Broomall, PA 19008
www.masoncrest.com

Copyright © 2014 by Mason Crest, an imprint of National Highlights, Inc. All rights reserved. No part of this publication may be reproduced or transmitted in any form or by any means, electronic or mechanical, including photocopying, recording, taping or any information storage and retrieval system, without permission from the publisher.

Printed and bound in the United States of America.

First printing
9 8 7 6 5 4 3 2 1

Series ISBN: 978-1-4222-2874-6
Hardcover ISBN: 978-1-4222-2878-4
ebook ISBN: 978-1-4222-8940-2
Paperback ISBN: 978-1-4222-2992-7

The Library of Congress has cataloged the
    hardcopy format(s) as follows:

Library of Congress Cataloging-in-Publication Data

Etingoff, Kim.
  Healthy alternatives to sweets & snacks / Kim Etingoff.
      pages cm. – (Understanding nutrition : a gateway to physical & mental health)
  Audience: Grade 4 to 6.
  ISBN 978-1-4222-2878-4 (hardcover) – ISBN 978-1-4222-2874-6 (series) – ISBN 978-1-4222-2992-7 (paperback) – ISBN 978-1-4222-8940-2 (ebook)
 1. Children–Nutrition–Juvenile literature. 2. Snack foods–Juvenile literature. 3. Nutrition–Juvenile literature. 4. Health–Nutrition–Juvenile literature. I. Title. II. Title: Healthy alternatives to sweets and snacks.
  TX355.E86 2014
  641.5'622–dc23
                              2013009799

Produced by Vestal Creative Services.
www.vestalcreative.com

Understanding Nutrition
A Gateway to Physical & Mental Health

Healthy Alternatives to Sweets & Snacks

Kim Etingoff

Mason Crest

Contents

Introduction	6
1. Sweets and Treats	9
2. Sugar, Salt, and Fats	17
3. Healthy Eating, Healthy Choices	27
4. Healthy Snacks	37
Find Out More	46
Index	47
About the Author & Consultant and Picture Credits	48

Introduction
by Dr. Joshua Borus

There are many decisions to make about food. Almost everyone wants to "eat healthy"—but what does that really mean? What is the "right" amount of food and what is a "normal" portion size? Do I need sports drinks if I'm an athlete—or is water okay? Are all "organic" foods healthy? Getting reliable information about nutrition can be confusing. All sorts of restaurants and food makers spend billions of dollars trying to get you to buy their products, often by implying that a food is "good for you" or "healthy." Food packaging has unbiased, standardized nutrition labels, but if you don't know what to look for, they can be hard to understand. Magazine articles and the Internet seem to always have information about the latest fad diets or new "superfoods" but little information you can trust. Finally, everyone's parents, friends, and family have their own views on what is healthy. How are you supposed to make good decisions with all this information when you don't know how to interpret it?

The goal of this series is to arm you with information to help separate what is healthy from not healthy. The books in the series will help you think about things like proper portion size and how eating well can help you stay healthy, improve your mood, and manage your weight. These books will also help you take action. They will let you know some of the changes you can make to keep healthy and how to compare eating options.

Keep in mind a few broad rules:

- First, healthy eating is a lifelong process. Learning to try new foods, preparing foods in healthy ways, and focusing on the big picture are essential parts of that process. Almost no one can keep on a very restrictive diet for a long time or entirely cut out certain groups of foods, so it's best to figure out how to eat healthy in a way that's realistic for you by making a number of small changes.

- Second, a lot of healthy eating hasn't really changed much over the years and isn't that complicated once you know what to look for. The core of a healthy diet is still eating reasonable portions at regular meals. This should be mostly fruits and vegetables, reasonable amounts of proteins, and lots of whole grains, with few fried foods or extra fats. "Junk food" and sweets also have their place—they taste good and have a role in celebrations and other happy events—but they aren't meant to be a cornerstone of your diet!
- Third, avoid drinks with calories in them, beverages like sodas, iced tea, and most juices. Try to make your liquid intake all water and you'll be better off.
- Fourth, eating shouldn't be done mindlessly. Often people will munch while they watch TV or play games because it's something to do or because they're bored rather then because they are hungry. This can lead to lots of extra food intake, which usually isn't healthy. If you are eating, pay attention, so that you are enjoying what you eat and aware of your intake.
- Finally, eating is just one part of the equation. Exercise every day is the other part. Ideally, do an activity that makes you sweat and gets your heart beating fast for an hour a day—but even making small decisions like taking stairs instead of elevators or walking home from school instead of driving make a difference.

After you read this book, don't stop. Find out more about healthy eating. Choosemyplate.gov is a great Internet resource from the U.S. government that can be trusted to give good information; www.hsph.harvard.edu/nutritionsource is a webpage from the Harvard School of Public Health where scientists sort through all the data about food and nutrition and distill it into easy-to-understand messages. Your doctor or nurse can also help you learn more about making good decisions. You might also want to meet with a nutritionist to get more information about healthy living.

Food plays an important role in social events, informs our cultural heritage and traditions, and is an important part of our daily lives. It's not just how we fuel our bodies; it's also but how we nourish our spirit. Learn how to make good eating decisions and build healthy eating habits—and you'll have increased long-term health, both physically and psychologically.

So get started now!

1

Sweets and Treats

We're supposed to eat three meals a day: breakfast, lunch, and dinner. But what about the in-between times? Just because it's not a mealtime doesn't mean you're not hungry. The in-between times are when you eat snacks.

Snacks are small amounts of food eaten between meals. They aren't as big as meals. They're meant to hold you over until you can eat a whole meal in a few hours.

Why Do We Snack?

Most of us snack because we're hungry! We feel that familiar rumbling in our stomachs, and we start chowing down.

In our culture, snacking is normal. When we feel hungry, we reach for a little something to eat. Even sometimes when we don't feel that hungry, but we just feel like eating, we have a snack. Maybe we're bored. Or lonely. Or worried. Snacking seems to make us feel better.

Snacks become habits. When you come home from school, you probably don't even stop to think about whether you're hungry or not. You just go to the cupboard or refrigerator to pull out something to eat. Maybe an evening snack before bedtime is normal, or a snack at school before lunch.

In other cultures, snacking isn't so common. Most people just eat at meals.

Even in the United States forty years ago, snacking wasn't as common as it is today. Today, we eat a lot more snacks than we used to. Most kids eat around three snacks everyday. In the 1970s, kids only ate one snack a day.

Sometimes it seems like people never stop eating! When it's not time for a meal, it's time for a snack.

Why Should We Snack?

Snacking can definitely be part of a healthy diet. Snacks sneak in some good food we don't get to eat at meals. Let's say you had cereal and milk for breakfast, a ham and vegetable sandwich for lunch with milk, and a stir-fry with tofu and vegetables for dinner. All of that is healthy food. But where's the fruit? You didn't eat any fruit for your meals. But between breakfast and lunch you could eat a banana. Between lunch and dinner you could have a berry smoothie. You just added a lot of fruit to your day with snacks!

> ### What Are Nutrients?
>
> **Nutrients** are the things in food that our bodies need in order to grow and stay alive.

Young people especially need to snack. They need a lot of **nutrients** to grow. Snacks are a good way to get those nutrients between meal times.

Snacks also keep us going. Have you ever felt shaky or cranky when you get hungry? Or gotten a headache? When people get hungry, it can be a really unpleasant feeling. Our bodies need food for energy. Eating a snack between meals helps give them the energy they need. You're happier and feel better when you eat a small snack.

For kids, snacks provide energy. After an afternoon of running around with friends, you're ready for some food even if it's not dinner time. A snack will give you that extra bit of energy you need to keep going until the next meal.

Snacks Today

Snacks are everywhere! Your cupboard is full of them at home. You can buy them at school. Malls have vending machines and fast-food restaurants. Whenever you want to eat, you can find a snack somewhere.

We're eating more snacks—but the problem is, we're also eating more unhealthy snacks. Eating too many unhealthy snacks is making people gain weight.

Unfortunately, most of the snacks we eat today are junk food. The three snacks a day young people normally eat are made up of candy, chips, ice cream, and crackers. These aren't healthy foods. They aren't adding good stuff to our **diets**.

Humans gain weight when they eat too much food. We need food every day to keep us going, but too much food makes us sick and it makes us gain weight.

About one-fifth of the people in the entire world are overweight or obese. Overweight means weighing a little too much. Obese means weighing a lot too much. In other words, around the world, one out of five people weigh too much. In areas of the world like Europe and most of North America, one out of two people are overweight or obese. That means half of all the people who live in those areas need to lose weight. More and more people all around the world have this problem. And it's a big problem because being overweight or obese makes people get sick more easily.

> ## What Are Diets?
>
> **Diets** can be a set of special rules for eating. Lots of times when people say they are *on a diet*, they mean they're following special rules that will help them lose weight. But diets can also mean the food we usually eat. Your diet is whatever you eat every day.

Sweets and Treats

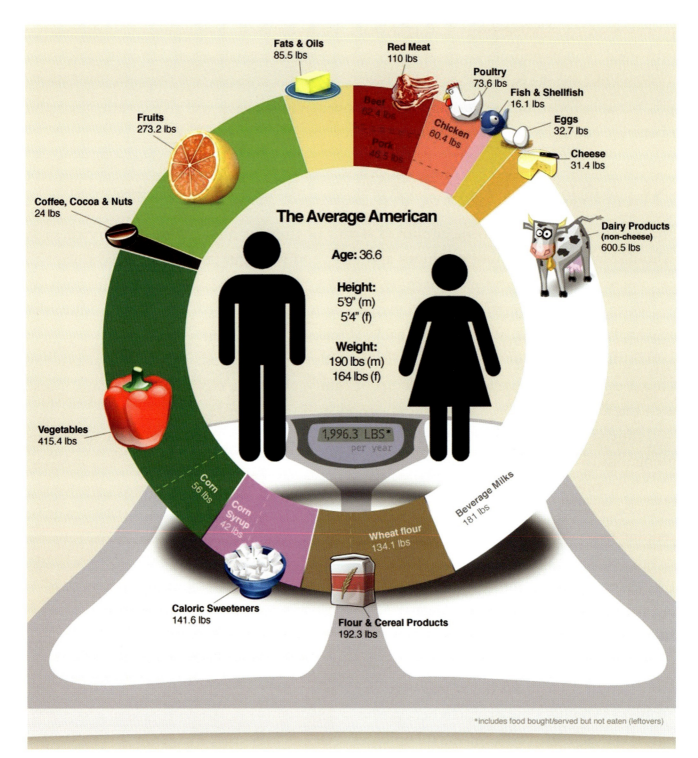

This chart shows what the average American eats each year. The average American eats 29 pounds of french fries, 23 pounds of pizza, and 24 pounds of ice cream each year.

12 Healthy Alternatives to Sweets & Snacks

Eating too many sweet or salty snacks can lead to weight gain and health problems. Try exchanging an unhealthy snack like chips or cookies with a piece of fruit.

Eating too much at meals is part of the problem. But snacks are another part of the problem. Because people eat snacks all the time, they start to gain weight.

Weight gain is unhealthy for a lot of reasons. Weight gain can make it hard for people to move around. Young people who weigh more are also more at risk for feeling bad about themselves. They are more at risk for **depression** too. As people continue to gain weight, they might face other health problems.

For example, weight gain leads to diabetes. Diabetes is a disease that messes with

What's Depression?

Everyone feels sad sometimes, but **depression** is when someone feels sad almost all the time. She may not feel like she has the energy to do the things she needs to do in a day. She may feel hopeless. Depression is a mental illness. When someone has depression, he needs help from a doctor or a psychiatrist.

Sweets and Treats

People with diabetes must regularly check how much sugar is in their blood, and be careful of when and what they eat.

> ### What Are Strokes?
>
> **Strokes** are when the blood flow in the brain is interrupted, so that brain cells don't get oxygen and die. When that happens, other parts of the body will no longer work normally. A person might not be able to speak normally or move parts of their bodies. Strokes can also cause death.

the insulin in the body. Insulin is a substance that helps the body use energy from food, specifically energy from carbohydrates (like sugar). People with diabetes have to watch what they eat and get a lot of exercise. Diabetes can also lead to serious problems, such as kidney failure and eye and nerve damage. Even young people are at risk for diabetes. More kids are getting diabetes these days.

Weight gain causes a lot of trouble for adults too. People who are overweight or obese are more likely to have heart problems, **strokes**, and joint and bone problems.

So the choice is up to you: feel healthy, strong, and happy for a lifetime by eating healthy now and in the future—or risk being overweight or obese by forming unhealthy eating habits. Choosing to eat healthy means choosing to be a better you.

Two Types of Diabetes

Diabetes actually comes in two types. Type 1 diabetes doesn't really have anything to do with a person's weight. The body doesn't make enough insulin, which is a serious condition. People with type 1 diabetes usually find out they have this disease when they are kids. There isn't any cure, but people with type 1 diabetes give themselves shots of insulin and watch what they eat carefully. Many more people have type 2 diabetes. Anyone at any age can be diagnosed with type 2 diabetes. Type 2 is tied to weight gain. People with type 2 diabetes don't usually have to give themselves shots. However, type 2 diabetes is also a serious disease.

2

Sugar, Salt, and Fats

Unhealthy snacks have three unhealthy things in them: sugar, salt, and unhealthy fats.

Sugar, salt, and fat aren't always bad things. They are all nutrients. Nutrients are substances we need to eat for our bodies to work right. Other nutrients include vitamins, protein, calcium, and potassium. We actually do need some sugar, salt, and fat every day.

We only need a little bit of each, though. We get in trouble when we eat too much of them. Eating so many unhealthy snacks is one way we end up with too much sugar, salt, and fat.

Sugar

So many of the things we eat and drink have sugar in them. Soda has a lot. So do sugary cereals, cookies, and candy. Even not very sweet things like bread and ketchup have sugar in them.

When we want a snack, many of us reach for something sweet. Sugary foods are hard to resist! They just taste so good.

Eating a little bit of sugar every day is okay. Your body needs some sugar. Sugar is a kind of carbohydrate, one of the nutrients in food. Carbohydrates give us energy and keep us going. Starch, fiber, and sugar are all kinds of carbohydrates.

Most of us end up eating too much sugar, though. Although we need a little sugar, too much can make us sick. We don't need to eat extremely sugary foods to get the sugar we need. Fruit has sugar in it, for example. Just eating fruit every day provides enough sugar.

Have you ever had a lot of sugar all at once? You probably got a lot of energy right away. Then you crashed a little while later. Maybe you even got a headache or a stomachache from eating so much sugar.

Too much sugar over time can lead to all sorts of bad things. Weight gain is one result. Scientists think eating sugar also may lead to diabetes, heart disease, and even **cancer**.

What Is Cancer?

Most everyone knows that **cancer** is a serious disease, but we don't always understand what cancer does to make a person sick. Cancer is a disease where the cells inside the body start reproducing too fast. This can make a tumor grow. The tumor can get in the way of healthy body cells doing their jobs. As cancer spreads throughout the body, it can damage more and more healthy parts.

Salt

Other snack foods are high in salt. Chips especially have a lot of salt. So do pretzels, popcorn, cheese sauce, and pickles.

Again, we do need some salt. Our bodies use salt—in the form of sodium—to balance how much water is in our cells. Sodium helps us sweat and keeps our body cool. A little bit of sodium every day is a good thing.

Facts from the American Diabetes Association

Total: 25.8 million children and adults in the United States—8.3% of the population—have diabetes.

Diagnosed: 18.8 million people

Undiagnosed: 7.0 million people

Prediabetes: 79 million people

New Cases: 1.9 million new cases of diabetes are diagnosed in people aged 20 years and older in 2010.

Under 20 years of age:
215,000, or 0.26% of all people in this age group have diabetes. About 1 in every 400 children and adolescents has diabetes.

But too much, just like too much sugar, is unhealthy. Kids only need 1,000 to 1,500 milligrams of sodium a day. The amount of sodium you need is about the weight of a pen cap. But most young people eat way more than 1,500 milligrams of sodium. Some people regularly eat five times the amount of sodium they should every day! Snacks are a big culprit. They add in all that salt you don't need.

Sugar, Salt, and Fats

Too much salt can cause heart problems. It can cause high blood pressure. Even though salty foods taste so good, eating them isn't worth all the health problems they can cause.

How Much Sodium?

Check out how much sodium (salt) is in some common snack foods. The less sodium, the better. All sizes represent how much of each snack a person might be most likely to eat for a snack.

Small package pretzel sticks: 260 milligrams
Small bag plain potato chips: 210 milligrams
26 tortilla chips: 240 milligrams
22 sour cream and onion chips: 300 milligrams
1 oz. salted mixed nuts: 95 milligrams

Fat

The third unhealthy thing snack foods have in them is fat. Not all fats are unhealthy, though. Some are healthier than others.

Healthy fats are called unsaturated fats. Avocados, nuts, and vegetable oils have unsaturated fats in them. Unsaturated fats can make your heart healthier. They transport vitamins in your body and help your immune system fight disease.

Unhealthy fats are called saturated fats and trans fats. Meat, dairy, eggs, and coconuts have saturated fat in them. You don't have to stop eating these foods because they have saturated fat. Instead, you should limit how much of them you eat.

Dietary Fat

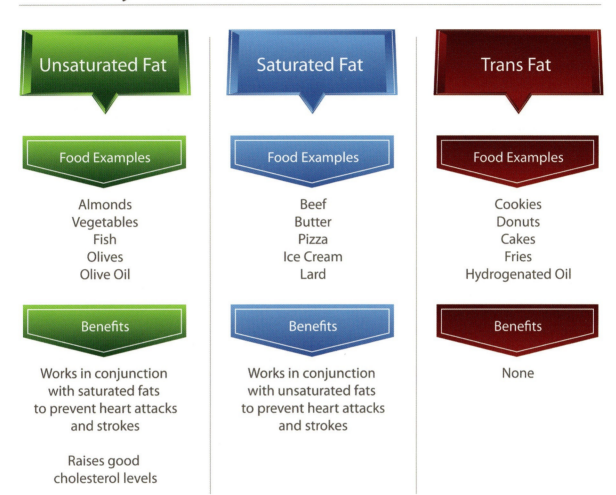

The three different kinds of dietary fat are in different foods and have very different effects on the body.

Saturated fats make your heart unhealthy, the opposite of unsaturated fats. They cause high blood pressure, heart attacks, and strokes.

Most trans fats are made in factories. You'll find trans fats in processed foods and fried foods. French fries, donuts, and cookies often have trans fats. Margarine often has trans fat in it. Look on packages for the ingredient list. If you see "partially hydrogenated oil" on the list, that means trans fat.

Sugar, Salt, and Fats

Trans fats are the least healthy fats. They raise your risk of heart disease the most. Luckily, many food companies and restaurants have figured out that trans fats are unhealthy. They label them now, or they have replaced them.

Processed versus Real Food

A healthy-eating guideline is to eat as much real food as possible. Real food is simple food that hasn't been made at a factory. Real foods only have one or two ingredients. Milk is milk. Grapes are grapes. Oats are oats. You can use real foods to make your own homemade meals. For example, you can make oats into oatmeal with honey and raisins on top (two other real foods).

Another good healthy-eating guideline is to limit how many processed foods you eat. Processed foods are made in factories. Processed foods have a lot more ingredients in them. They also have a lot of sugar, salt, and fat. Store-bought cake, cereal, canned soup, and boxed macaroni and cheese are all processed foods.

Reading Food Labels for Sugar, Salt, and Fat

You don't just have to guess whether a food has a lot of sugar, salt, or fat. You can look at the food label, which will tell you!

Food labels are the black-and-white charts on the back or sides of almost all packaged foods. Food labels list different parts of the food, and how much of each is in the food.

First, look for the part of the food label that says "carbohydrates." Some food labels will list sugar underneath carbohydrates. The label will list sugar in grams. A

INGREDIENTS: CULTURED GRADE A REDUCED FAT MILK, APPLES, HIGH FRUCTOSE CORN SYRUP, CINNAMON, NUTMEG, NATURAL FLAVORS, AND PECTIN. CONTAINS ACTIVE YOGURT AND L. ACIDOPHILUS CULTURES.

Try to stay away from foods that are made with high fructose corn syrup, a type of sugar. Many sugary snacks and drinks are made with the unhealthy syrup, so be sure to check the nutrition facts to see what your next snack is made of and see if you can make a healthier choice.

food with 24 grams of sugar is very high in sugar. A food with just 1 gram of sugar is fairly low.

Take a look at the ingredient list next to the nutrition table. Stay away from snacks that list sugar as one of the first ingredients. The list might say: sugar, high fructose corn syrup, cane juice, fructose, glucose, maltose, or sucrose. All those words mean sugar!

Next, look for the part of the food label that says sodium. Sodium is a way to measure how much salt is in a food. Labels measure sodium in milligrams. Look for foods that are low sodium, with less than 140 milligrams of sodium. Even less is better.

You'll also see a percentage under sodium. You should get 100 percent of the sodium you need every day. The food you're eating has a certain percentage. If you eat something with 50 percent of your daily sodium, you've just eaten half of all the sodium you need in just one food! Keep your percentages low and you won't go overboard.

Look for the part of the food label that says fat. The label lists different kinds of fats, like saturated and trans fats. Fats are measured in grams. Eat foods that are low in all these

Sugar, Salt, and Fats

Nutrition Facts

Serving Size 1 container (227g)

Amount Per Serving

Calories 240 Calories from Fat 25

	% Daily Value*
Total Fat 3g	4 %
Saturated Fat 1.5g	9 %
Trans Fat 0g	
Cholesterol 15mg	5 %
Sodium 140mg	6 %
Total Carbohydrate 46g	15 %
Dietary Fiber Less than 1g	3 %
Sugars 44g	
Protein 9g	
Vitamin A 2 % • Vitamin C	4 %
Calcium 35 % • Iron	0 %

*Percent Daily Values are based on a 2,000 calorie diet. Your Daily Values may be higher or lower depending on your calorie needs.

Checking the nutrition facts is the best way to find out how much fat, salt, and sugar is in the food you eat.

HEALTHY ALTERNATIVES TO SWEETS & SNACKS

fats, especially saturated and trans fats. Don't eat more than 1 or 2 grams of saturated or trans fats in one food.

Once you learn how to read a food label, use it as a tool to help you eat healthy foods. With practice, you'll be able to tell what's a healthy food and what isn't.

3

Healthy Eating, Healthy Choices

Choosing healthy snacks seems like a good idea, but how do you do it? What should you eat? What should you stay away from?

You're better off thinking about healthy eating guidelines, rather than rules. Healthy eating will look a little different for different people. For example, one person might not feel very good when they eat a lot of meat. Another person feels great and has a lot of energy when they eat meat every day. Eating less meat is healthier for the first person. Eating more meat is healthier for the second.

Healthy eating guidelines aren't that complicated. Eat more fruits and vegetables. Eat whole grains and proteins. Eat a variety of foods. Limit how many processed foods you eat with lots of salt, sugar, and unhealthy fat.

Whole-grain bread is much healthier than white bread. Though some diets suggest giving up all carbohydrates (including those in bread), the carbs in whole-grain bread are better for you than those in white bread.

HEALTHY ALTERNATIVES TO SWEETS & SNACKS

Eat More Fruits and Vegetables

You can make your diet a lot healthier just by eating more fruits and vegetables. Basically, fruits and vegetables have a lot of good stuff in them, and not a lot bad stuff.

Fruits and vegetables have good nutrients. Nutrients are substances our bodies need to work right. They make bones strong, help muscles grow, help us see, give us energy, and a lot more besides. Without nutrients, people get sick.

You've probably heard of some nutrients, like vitamins and minerals. Calcium, iron, and potassium are all examples of minerals. Carbohydrates are a kind of nutrient. Fats and proteins are too.

Fruits and vegetables in particular have a lot of vitamins and minerals. When we eat them, we get the benefit of those nutrients.

Fresh fruits and vegetables are the best choice. They have a lot of nutrients, and they taste great! Bananas, apples, kiwis, grapes, and more are great fruit snacks. Carrots, celery, and broccoli are good vegetable choices.

Frozen fruits and vegetables are good choices too. They're less easy to use for snacks, but they are good options for meals because they still have lots of nutrients. Make frozen fruit into smoothies for a snack drink!

Canned fruits and vegetables are the next-best choice. Some canned fruit is packed in syrup. That syrup has a lot of extra sugar in it. Fruit has enough natural sugar in it—you don't have to add any more! Canned vegetables sometimes have extra salt. Check the nutrition label for extra sugar or high levels of sodium. Choose cans that are filled with just fruit and just vegetables.

Eat Whole Grains

Grains are the seeds of grass plants. Rice is a grain, and so are wheat, oats, and barley. We eat a lot of foods made out of grains, especially wheat. Wheat is ground up into flour, and flour is made into bread and lots of baked goods.

Each grain seed has three parts. All three parts have nutrients in them, like protein and vitamins. Refined grains—non-whole grains—have two parts taken out. Factories take them out so the grains will last longer on grocery store shelves and at home. But the grains

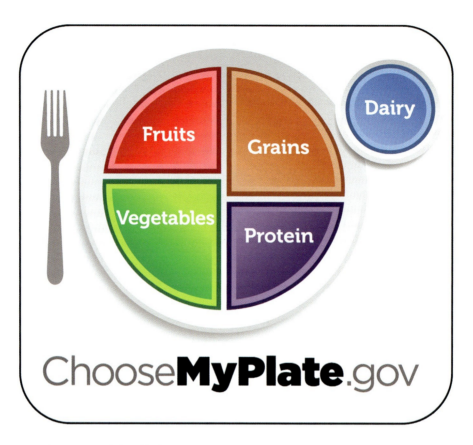

Governments around the world tell their people about healthy eating in different ways. In the United States, MyPlate shows Americans how much of each kind of food they should eat in each meal.

also lose some of their nutrients. Whole grains still have all three parts. They also have all the nutrients, which makes them healthier.

Foods made out of whole grains are generally better for you than foods made out of non-whole grains. Choose whole-grain foods like brown rice, oats, millet, quinoa, and whole-wheat products. Whole-grain foods are usually darker than refined foods. You might think you don't like them—but give them a try!

Vary Your Foods

We usually divide food up into food groups. Fruits are a food group, along with vegetables. Grains are another group.

Dairy is another food group. Dairy includes milk, cheese, and yogurt. Anything made from animal milk counts as dairy. Dairy has healthy fats, calcium, vitamins, and more good nutrients.

Proteins are a big food group. Protein is a nutrient that helps you grow strong and keeps your muscles healthy. Meat has a lot of protein in it, but there are other sources of protein too. Beans, tofu, and nuts are all good sources of protein.

Try to eat food from as many different food groups as you can. In one day, you should eat food from all five food groups. Even in each group, vary what you eat. Don't just eat meat for protein. Try beans and lentils too.

Every food has a different set of nutrients. The way to get as many of those nutrients as possible is to eat many different foods as possible. For instance, a balanced breakfast might have four food groups: a grapefruit (fruit), whole-wheat toast (grain) with peanut butter (protein), and a glass of milk (dairy).

Eat Your Colors

Think of varying your fruits and vegetables by color! Eat a rainbow, and you'll be as healthy as you can be. Every color of fruit and vegetable helps a different part of your body. Red (tomatoes, apples, and watermelon) helps the heart and circulatory system. Orange and yellow helps your eyes, so eat carrots, oranges, and pineapple. Green (kale, green peppers, and avocados) keeps your bones strong. Blue and purple fruits and veggies keep your brain healthy and help you remember things, so eat blueberries, eggplants, and purple cabbage. White and brown work with your digestive system, so eat potatoes, onions, and cauliflower. Of course, every color fruit and vegetable helps keep you healthy in more ways than one. Eat them all to get the full effect!

Healthy Eating, Healthy Choices

Snacking on fruit will always be healthier than picking up a bag of chips or cookies. Switching an unhealthy snack for a healthier one is a great way to limit your junk food and the number of calories you eat.

Healthy Alternatives to Sweets & Snacks

Limit Junk Food

Healthy eating isn't just about eating good food—it's also about limiting unhealthy foods.

Unhealthy foods don't have many good nutrients. They do have a lot of sugar, salt, and unhealthy fats. Unhealthy foods just fill you up, but they don't give you any good nutrients.

Some unhealthy foods are called junk foods. We eat junk foods as snacks a lot. Junk foods are the familiar chips, candy, and other processed foods we sometimes eat as snacks.

No food is so bad you can never eat it. Even unhealthy foods are okay to eat once in a while. The trick is to limit how much of them you eat. Instead of eating french fries every other day, eat them twice a month. Save cake for special occasions like birthday parties.

Keep Calories in Check

All food has calories. Calories are just the way we measure how much energy food has, and all food has energy. Energy is the reason we eat food in the first place. Energy gets us up in the morning, keeps us moving, and makes sure our bodies can breathe and pump blood.

You can measure food in a lot of different ways. You could measure how long a piece of spinach is in inches. You could weigh it in grams. And you could measure how much energy it has in calories.

Calories aren't bad. Everyone needs calories to live. In fact, we all need about 2,000 calories every day. Some people need a little more or a little fewer, but 2,000 is a good average. This means the calories in every food you eat in a day should add up to about 2,000. Our bodies use up 2,000 calories a day. If we eat more than that, we start to gain weight. Eating fewer than 2,000 calories leads to weight loss.

People gain weight because they eat too many calories. Snacks are one way people sneak in extra calories in their diet. Eating big snacks, or too many snacks, adds calories you don't really need. Your body stores those calories as fat. Over time, the extra calories add on pounds.

1 Serving Looks Like . . .

Grain Products

1 cup of cereal flakes = fist

1 pancake = compact disc

½ cup of cooked rice, pasta, or potato = ½ baseball

1 slice of bread = cassette tape

1 piece of cornbread = bar of soap

1 Serving Looks Like . . .

Vegetables and Fruit

1 cup of salad greens = baseball

1 baked potato = fist

1 med. fruit = baseball

½ cup of fresh fruit = ½ baseball

¼ cup of raisins = large egg

1 Serving Looks Like . . .

Dairy and Cheese

1½ oz. cheese = 4 stacked dice or 2 cheese slices

½ cup of ice cream = ½ baseball

Fats

1 tsp. margarine or spreads = 1 dice

1 Serving Looks Like . . .

Meat and Alternatives

3 oz. meat, fish, and poultry = deck of cards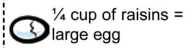

3 oz. grilled/baked fish = checkbook

2 Tbsp. peanut butter = ping pong ball

Paying attention to the size of a serving of your favorite foods is a great way to make sure you keep the number of calories you eat each day in check.

34 Healthy Alternatives to Sweets & Snacks

Not all calories are the same. Calories in foods that come packed with nutrients are great! When you get vitamins and minerals along with your 300-calorie meal, you're eating healthy. But unhealthy foods are unhealthy because their calories don't come with nutrients. Instead, they have a lot of empty calories. A bag of chips might have 200 calories, and a lot of salt, but that's it. The chips don't have many vitamins or minerals. Calories without nutrients are called empty calories.

Healthy eating guidelines apply to your life all the time. They work for eating at home, in restaurants, or at school. They work for meals—and they work for snack time!

4

Healthy Snacks

The next time you want to reach for a sugary, salty, or fatty snack, think again. Eat a healthy snack instead.

Nutritious Snacks

The guidelines for eating healthy snacks are the same as for eating healthy meals. Eat more fruits and vegetables. Choose whole grains. Eat a variety of foods. Here are some healthy snack suggestions you could try:

Vegetable Snacks

- Carrots and hummus dip. Buy hummus at the store, or make your own by blending chick peas, olive oil, and lemon juice.
- Ants on a log. Cut up celery sticks, fill them with peanut butter (or cream cheese) and put raisins on top.
- Homemade guacamole with tortilla chips. Smash up half an avocado with lime juice. Use the oven to toast triangles made out of whole wheat or corn tortillas.

Fruit Snacks

- A fresh banana, orange, kiwi, or mango. Whole pieces of fruit or cut-up fruit slices are good for home or on the go.
- Apples slices and nut butter. Cut up apples and stick them in peanut, almond, or sunflower butter.
- Applesauce. Buy low-sugar applesauce or make your own.
- Dried fruit, like raisins, figs, or cranberries. Mix them up with nuts, coconut, and a few chocolate chips for trail mix.
- Frozen grapes or bananas. Place whole grapes or banana slices in the freezer and pop them in your mouth after a few hours—almost like ice cream!

Grains Snacks

- Mini pizza on a whole-wheat English muffin. Cut muffins in half, spread tomato sauce, cheese, and veggies on top, then toast in the oven for a few minutes.
- Whole-wheat mini banana muffin. Make muffins with bananas, nuts, and whole-wheat flour in mini muffin tins.
- Small bowl of oatmeal. Mix oats with water or milk, cook, and serve with honey, dried fruit, yogurt, or nuts.
- Air-popped popcorn. Skip the store-bought bagged popcorn, and pop your own on the stove or in a brown paper bag in the microwave.

Dairy Snacks

- Plain yogurt mixed with honey and fruit. Flavored yogurt usually has a lot of sugar, but you can make your own version at home.

Fruit salad is a healthy, easy-to-make snack that you can eat at home or at school. If you make a lot all at once, you'll have a healthy snack for a few days.

Healthy Snacks

- Whole-grain crackers and cheese. Slice up a little bit of cheddar or gouda and spread on crackers.
- Fresh fruit smoothie. Blend frozen fruit (or fresh, along with an ice cube) with milk or juice.

Protein Snacks

- Roasted nuts. Buy lightly salted roasted nuts, or make your own in the oven.
- Hard-boiled egg. Boil an egg for seven to eight minutes to make sure the yolk inside is hard.
- Turkey and vegetables in a whole-wheat tortilla. Spread a tortilla with cream cheese or hummus, your favorite meat and veggies, and roll up into a wrap.

In general, it's better to make your own snacks instead of buying bags or boxes of them. For example, if you make your own applesauce, you can control what's in there. Just cook up some apples in a pot, add a little sugar and cinnamon, and you're all set! The applesauce you buy in the store might have lots more sugar than you need.

When you know you're going to be traveling, keep some healthy snacks with you. On a trip to the mall, take some baby carrots or whole grain crackers. You'll be less tempted to go to the vending machine and get some candy instead. Take healthy snacks with you in the car if you're going on a long car trip too.

Healthy snack possibilities are endless! Be creative, and you can make snack time fun.

What About "All-Natural" Snacks?

Packages that say the food inside is "natural" may seem healthier. But that's not always the case. The word "natural" doesn't really mean anything. Any food company can use it if they want—it's just a way to get people to buy their product. Foods labeled as natural can still have lots of sugar, salt, fat, and other stuff in there. Check the label to see if a natural snack really is healthy.

Soybeans (sometimes called edamame when cooked) are a tasty and healthy snack packed with plenty of protein. For vegetarians or vegans, soybeans can be a good way to get protein from food that doesn't come from animals.

Healthy Snacks 41

Many people eat while watching TV; turning on their favorite show just isn't the same without a snack. If you notice the times you snack most, that can help you to limit your snacking.

Snacking Less

Even if your snacks are pretty healthy, you could still get in to trouble by eating too many snacks. Learn to eat snacks only when you really need them.

Snacking can become a bad habit. Breaking the habit is the hard part. After that, you'll find it easier to keep from snacking when you don't really need a snack.

The first step to beating your snack habit is to figure out when you snack too much. Think about all the times you normally snack. You can even write them down if you want to. Do you snack right after school? While you're watching television? Before bed?

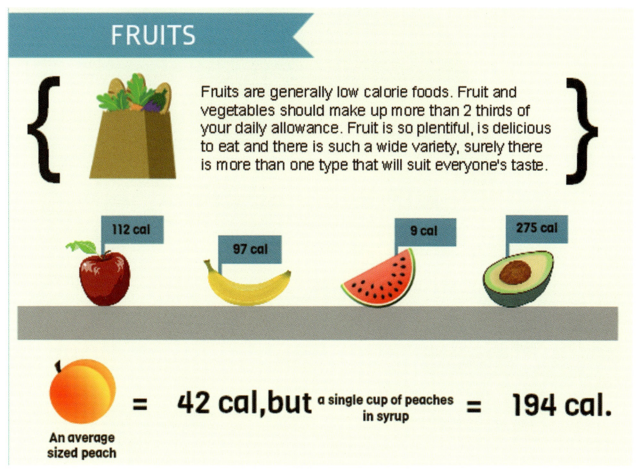

Remember that fresh fruit is a healthier snack than fruit in a can or cup, with fewer calories and added sugar.

How many of those snack times are right before or after a meal? You should cut out any snack times that are an hour before or after a meal. Before a meal, it's okay to be hungry! You don't always have to eat the minute you feel hungry. By waiting until the meal, you're making sure you're not filling up on snack foods before you eat your main dish. And eat enough during breakfast, lunch, and dinner so you don't get hungry again right away.

Also think about whether you're really hungry when you snack. Were you hungry when you grabbed a snack after school at your friend's house? Or were you just eating a snack because your friend was? If you find you're not hungry when you're eating snacks, cut them out.

Healthy Snacks

Choosing water over juice or soda is one of the best ways to cut down on calories, but drinking water when you feel hungry can also be a good way to keep from eating when you're really just thirsty.

Try not to eat more than two snacks a day—one between breakfast and lunch, and one between lunch and dinner, or a light snack in the evening. Too many snacks add up to too many calories.

Whenever you snack, sit at the kitchen table. Pay attention to what you're eating. A lot of the time, we overeat when we're not really paying attention to our food. Snacking while watching TV is an example of not paying attention to your food. You won't notice when you're full, and you'll keep eating more snack than you need.

Avoid eating snacks right out of the package. Instead of eating crackers from the box, measure out ten or fifteen and put them on a plate. People tend to overeat when they eat from packages and don't notice how much they've eaten.

Another good tip is to drink a glass of water every time you think you're hungry. A lot of the time when you think you feel hungry, you're actually thirsty. See if your body needs water rather than food, and drink water. Then, if you're still hungry, eat a snack. You'll be cutting out extra food you don't need, and giving your body the water it needs.

Make snacks a healthy part of your day. Skip unhealthy sugary, salty, and fatty snacks. When you feel hungry between meals, do yourself a favor—eat a healthy snack!

Healthy Snacks

Find Out More

ONLINE

Eat Right
www.eatright.org/nutritiontipsheets/#.URU9_VrhlAQ

KidsHealth: Smart Snacking
www.kidshealth.org/teen/food_fitness/nutrition/healthy_snacks.html

Let's Move! Kids
www.letsmove.gov/kids

Super Health Kids Snack Recipes
www.superhealthykids.com/healthy-kids-recipes/category/snacks.php

IN BOOKS

Claybourne, Anna. *Healthy Eating: Diet and Nutrition*. North Mankato, Minn.: Heinemann-Raintree, 2008.

La Monica, Gina. *Tid Bits: A Quick & Healthy Guide to Kids' Snacks*. Lompoc, Calif.: Summerland Publishing, 2010.

Mayo Clinic. *The Mayo Clinic Kids' Cookbook*. Intercourse, Penn.: Good Books, 2012.

Index

calorie(s) 7, 32–35, 43–45
carbohydrate(s) 14, 18, 22, 28–29
culture 10

dairy 20, 31, 38
diabetes 13–15, 18–19
diet(s) 6–7, 10–11, 21, 28–29, 33, 46

energy 11, 13–14, 18, 27, 29, 33

fat 7, 17, 20–25, 27, 29, 31, 33, 37, 40, 45
food group(s) 30, 31
food label(s) 22–23, 25
fruit(s) 7, 10, 13, 18, 27, 29–32, 37–40, 43

grain(s) 7, 27–31, 37–38, 40

habit(s) 7, 10, 15, 42
heart disease 18, 22

junk food 7, 11, 32–33

meal(s) 7, 9–11, 13, 22, 29, 35, 37, 45
minerals 29, 35

natural 29, 40
nutrient(s) 10, 17–18, 29–31, 33, 35

processed foods 21–22, 27, 33
protein(s) 7, 17, 27, 29, 31, 40–41

salt 13, 17–20, 22–24, 27, 29, 33, 35, 37, 40, 45
saturated fat(s) 20–21
sodium 18–20, 23, 29
sugar 14, 17–19, 22–24, 27, 29, 33, 37–38, 40, 43, 45

trans fat(s) 20–23, 25

unsaturated fat(s) 20–21

vegetable(s) 7, 10, 20, 27, 29–31, 37–38, 40
vitamins 17, 20, 29, 31, 35

water 6–7, 18, 31, 38, 44–45
weight 6, 11, 13–15, 18–19, 33
whole grain(s) 7, 27–30, 37, 40

About the Author & Consultant

Kim Etingoff lives in Boston, Massachusetts, spending part of her time working on farms. Kim has written a number of books for young people on topics including health, history, nutrition, and business.

Dr. Borus graduated from the Harvard Medical School and the Harvard School of Public Health. He completed a residency in Pediatrics and then served as Chief Resident at Floating Hospital for Children at Tufts Medical Center before completing a fellowship in Adolescent Medicine at Boston Children's Hospital. He is currently an attending physician in the Division of Adolescent and Young Adult Medicine at Boston Children's Hospital and an Instructor of Pediatrics at Harvard Medical School.

Picture Credits

ChooseMyPlate.gov: p. 30
Dreamstime.com:
    Ariwasabi: p.16
    Barbara Delgado-millea: p. 41
    Constantin Opris: p. 36
    Darren Baker: p. 39
    Jason Stitt: p. 13
    Jim Delillo: p. 14
    John Takai: p. 21
    Lev Kropotov: p. 44
    Monkey Business Images: p. 26, 32
    Slav8: p. 42
    Tab1962: p. 28
    Vaskoni: p. 8
United States Department of Agriculture: p. 34
visualeconomics.com: p. 10

To the best knowledge of the publisher, all other images are in the public domain. If any image has been inadvertently uncredited or miscredited, please notify Vestal Creative Services, Vestal, New York, 13850, so that rectification can be made for future printings.

j Greater Sudbury Public Library